THE CAN–DO KARATE KID

A Dojo Kun Character Book

On Defeating Laziness & Procrastination

by Jenifer Tull-Gauger

YOUTH LITERARY LEAGUE

Youth Literary League

www.JeniferTullGauger.com

KARATE WORDS
IN THIS STORY
(AND HOW TO PRONOUNCE FOR AMERICAN ENGLISH.):

dojo \ ˈdō-jō \: Japanese for place of the way. A training hall for a Japanese art like karate.

Dojo Kun \ ˈdō-jō ˈkün \: the creed or oath of the dojo. The most important rules of traditional karate, created by Shungo Sakugawa, a karate master from Okinawa.

gi \ ˈgē \: uniform worn in Japanese martial arts.

gi top \ ˈgē ˌtäp \: traditional fold-over martial arts shirt.

karate \ kə-ˈrä-tē \: Japanese for empty hand. The name given to the martial arts developed in Okinawa (formerly the Ryukyu Kingdom).

Renshi \ ˈren-ˌshē \: Japanese for expert teacher. A special title for a high-rank black belt instructor.

Sensei \ ˈsen-ˌsā \: Japanese for before born. Respectful title for a teacher.

CHARACTERS IN THIS BOOK

Makoto \ mə-ˈkō-tō \: Japanese for truth or sincerity. Also a name.

Michi \ ˈmē-chē \: Japanese for righteous way or good path. Also a name.

Laziness \ ˈlā-zē-nəs \: a form of lazy. Being unwilling to work, unwilling to use energy, slow-moving.

Procrastination \ prə-ˌkra-stə-ˈnā-shən \: to put off or delay something that must be done.

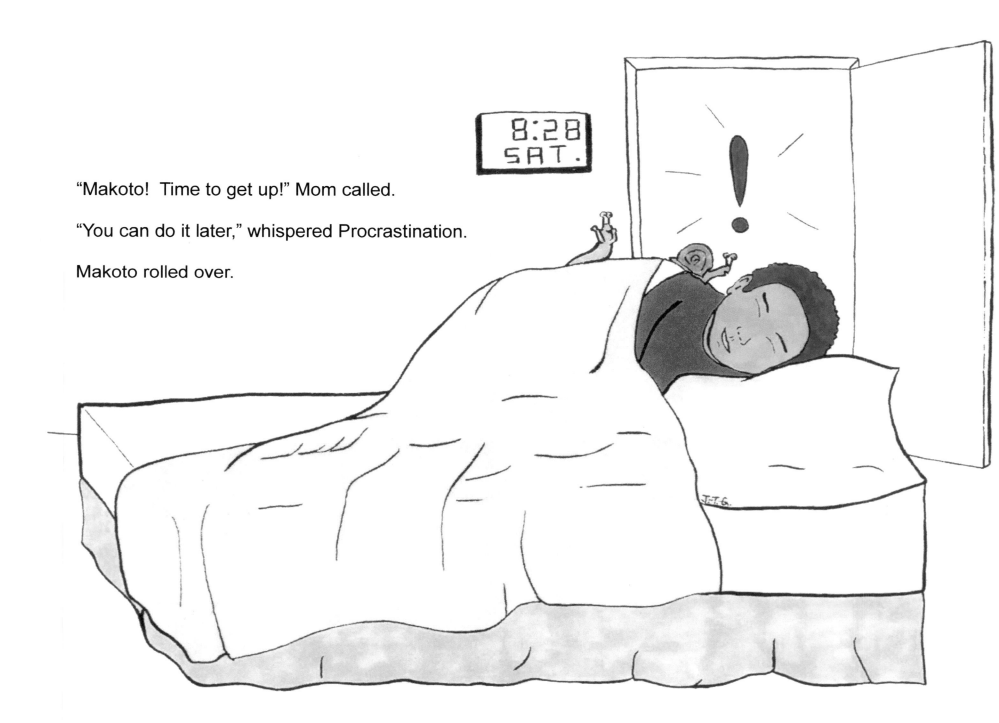

"Makoto! Time to get up!" Mom called.

"You can do it later," whispered Procrastination.

Makoto rolled over.

Mom's voice woke him again, "MAKOTO! Hurry up or you'll be LATE!"

Laziness said, "Why bother?"

Makoto lay there. Then he slowly sat up and went downstairs.

Dad said, "You might want to hurry. You have a belt test!"

Mom said, "Good morning, eat up!"

Laziness said, "Take your time."

Makoto took his time.

Mom said, "Are you done?" But Makoto was listening to Procrastination.

Mom talked louder, "Makoto! Are you through eating? It's time to go."

"Okay, I'm done," he said.

"Better hurry!" said Dad.

Makoto went with Laziness and Procrastination to get ready for the **dojo**.

On the way, Mom asked,

"Makoto, do you have your

karate top?"

He checked his bag, "Uh oh!"

"What?" said Dad.

Makoto said, "It's not here!"

Dad stopped the car.

"Makoto!" Dad yelled.

Are you sure?

Makoto looked again,

"It's not here."

Mom talked fast,

"I washed your **gi** for you.

I told you to put it in your bag.

Now you don't have the shirt?

What happened?"

"I don't know," said Makoto.

Yesterday Dad gave him the uniform while he watched TV.

He knew Laziness and Procrastination had something to do with this.

Dad said, "You'll be really late now. We have to go back and get it."

Mom said, "You might miss your test."

Makoto had an idea, "No, we don't have to go back. I can borrow a **gi top**!"

"Are you sure?" Mom asked.

He said, "**Sensei** let my friend Michi borrow one."

"Well, okay," said Dad. He drove the rest of the way to the dojo.

Inside, Makoto looked for Sensei.

But Sensei was up front with the other teachers.

Other students were taking their test.

Makoto stood at the side.

He didn't know what to do.

Makoto put his hands on the floor.

He knew that you have to do pushups when you are late to class.

Makoto was late a lot.

Renshi told him to stop. She was the head teacher.

Makoto sat down at the side.

His face was hot.

The instructors watched the
other students do their karate.

Michi was taking her test.

She looked over and
smiled at Makoto.

He sat still with his eyes stinging.

What should he do?

Laziness and Procrastination
were nowhere around.

When it was sparring gear time, Mike, the junior black belt, came over, "What happened?"

Makoto said, "I don't know, I was late. Then I forgot my gi top. Could I borrow one?"

Mike said, "You can't be late to test, man. It interrupts everything. You'll have to make it up next time."

When Makoto told his parents, they just sat there.

Dad said, "We're talking to Renshi. She'll know what to do."

Makoto couldn't breathe.

He was late, he couldn't test and his parents were upset.

What would Renshi say?

After the test, Mom, Dad, Renshi and Makoto sat down.

Makoto felt like a bug under a magnifying glass.

Dad said, "We don't know what to do with Makoto. He made himself late."

Mom told Renshi, "We tried to get Makoto here on time, but because of his own actions, he was late."

Dad said, "It's hard to get him to do chores or anything."

Renshi asked, "What about school?"

"It's the same at school," said Mom.

"He turns in his homework late," said Dad.

"He hardly even tries," said Mom, his grades are suffering."

Renshi looked at Makoto, "Why is this happening?"

Makoto said, "I… don't… know."

Renshi said, "Laziness and Procrastination are our two biggest enemies. You have to fight them."

Makoto asked, "How?"

Renshi asked, "How can you use your **Dojo Kun**?"

Makoto thought, "I can do my best in all that I do."

Renshi asked, "How can you do that?"

He said, "I can focus, stay on that path, and try every day."

Then she asked, "How can you do that?"

Makoto said, "I can do what my parents say, the first time they ask. I can use self discipline!"

"Yes!" said Renshi. "You have to get rid of Laziness and Procrastination before you test."

DOJO KUN

1. Strive for a good moral character.
2. Keep an honest and sincere way.
3. Cultivate perseverance or a will for striving.
4. Develop a respectful attitude.
5. Restrain my physical abilities through spiritual attainment.

When he got home, Makoto did his homework.

He read his whole reading book.

It was hard and took a long time.

But when he finished, Makoto felt great!

The next morning, it wasn't easy, but he got up the first time his mom asked.

When Makoto went to school, he moved his feet, warrior strong and martial artist quick.

He felt good and was on time.

He focused his eyes. He focused his mind. He focused his body. He used his best writing.

Makoto was proud to turn in his class work.

After many more days of working hard to use his Dojo Kun, Makoto was invited again to test.

Makoto was ready on his next test day.

He got there early and had his full uniform.

You could not see Laziness or Procrastination.

During the test Makoto worked hard and did his best with every move.

Earning that belt made him happier than any other test (so far).

After that, Laziness and Procrastination would sometimes challenge him to a re-match.

Makoto used his Dojo Kun to keep them away, and it worked every time.

DOJO KUN

1. Strive for a good moral character.

2. Keep an honest and sincere way.

3. Cultivate perseverance or a will for striving.

4. Develop a respectful attitude.

5. Restrain my physical abilities through spiritual attainment.

道場訓

一、人格完成に努める事
一、誠の道を守る事
一、努力の精神を養心事
一、礼儀を重んずる事
一、血気の勇を戒める事
二十八年三月二十七日 拳眞館

Thanks for reading! In the next Dojo Kun Character Book, both Michi and Makoto battle dishonesty.

CPSIA information can be obtained at www.ICGtesting.com
Printed in the USA
BVIW120608280519
548970BV00001B/3

PHILIPPE LEGENDRE

KIDS CAN DRAW

Farm Animals

Walter Foster Publishing, Inc.
23062 La Cadena Drive
Laguna Hills, CA 92653 USA
ISBN 1-56010-280-2

Attention Parents and Teachers

All children can draw a circle, a square, or a triangle…which means that they can also learn to draw a chicken, cow, or pig! The KIDS CAN DRAW learning method is easy and fun. Children will learn a technique and a vocabulary of shapes that will form the basis for all kinds of drawing.

Pictures are created by combining geometric shapes to form a mass of volumes and surfaces. From this stage, children can give character to their sketches with straight, curved, or broken lines.

With just a few strokes of the pencil, a farm animal will appear—and with the addition of color, the picture will be real work of art!

The KIDS CAN DRAW method offers a real apprenticeship in technique and a first look at composition, proportion, shapes, and lines. The simplicity of this method ensures that the pleasure of drawing is always the most important factor.

About Philippe Legendre

French painter, engraver, and illustrator, Philippe Legendre also runs a school of art for children aged 6–14 years. Legendre frequently spends time in schools and has developed this method of learning so that all children can discover the artist within themselves.

Helpful Tips

1. Each picture is made up of simple geometric shapes, which are illustrated at the top of the left-hand page. This is called the **Vocabulary of Shapes.** Encourage children to practice drawing each shape before starting their pictures.

2. Suggest children use a pencil to do their sketches. This way, if they don't like a particular shape, they can just erase it and try again.

3. A dotted line indicates that the line should be erased. Have children draw the whole shape and then erase the dotted part of the line.

4. Once children finish their drawings, they can color them with crayons, colored pencils, or felt-tip markers. They may want to go over the lines with a black pencil or pen.

Now let's get started!

Here's the round donkey in gray.

He starts each morning...

with a loud bray.

Donkey

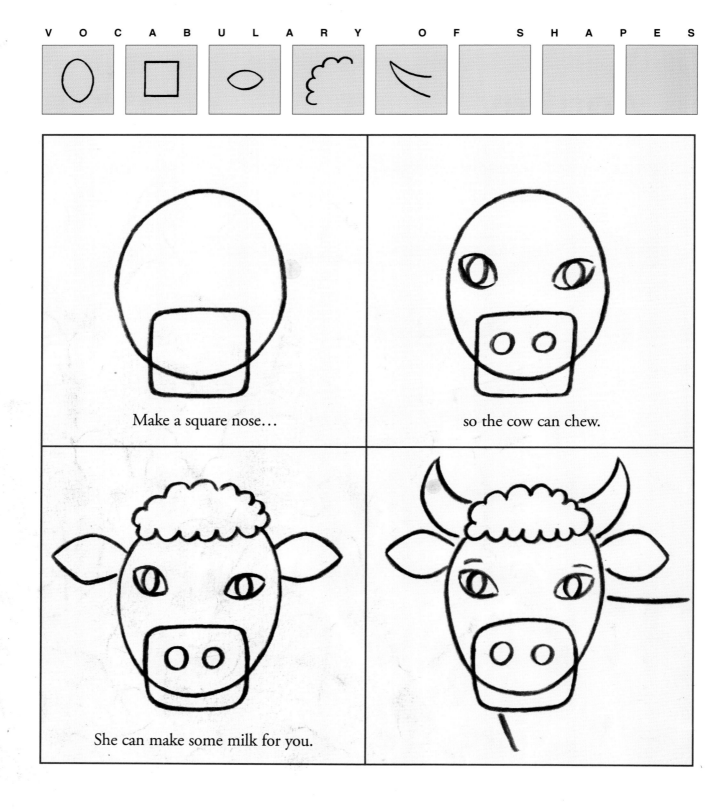

Make a square nose…

so the cow can chew.

She can make some milk for you.

Cow

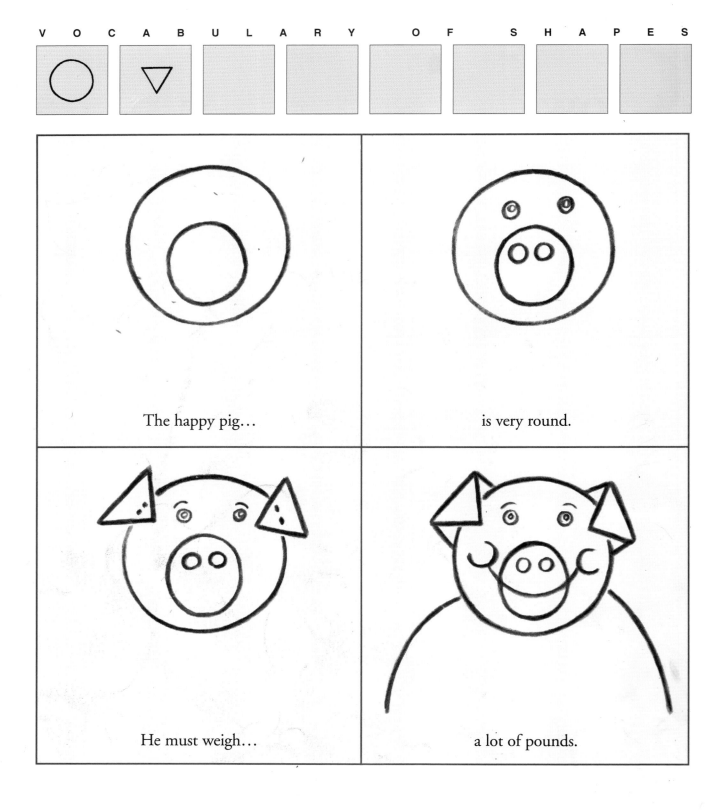

The happy pig…

is very round.

He must weigh…

a lot of pounds.

Pig

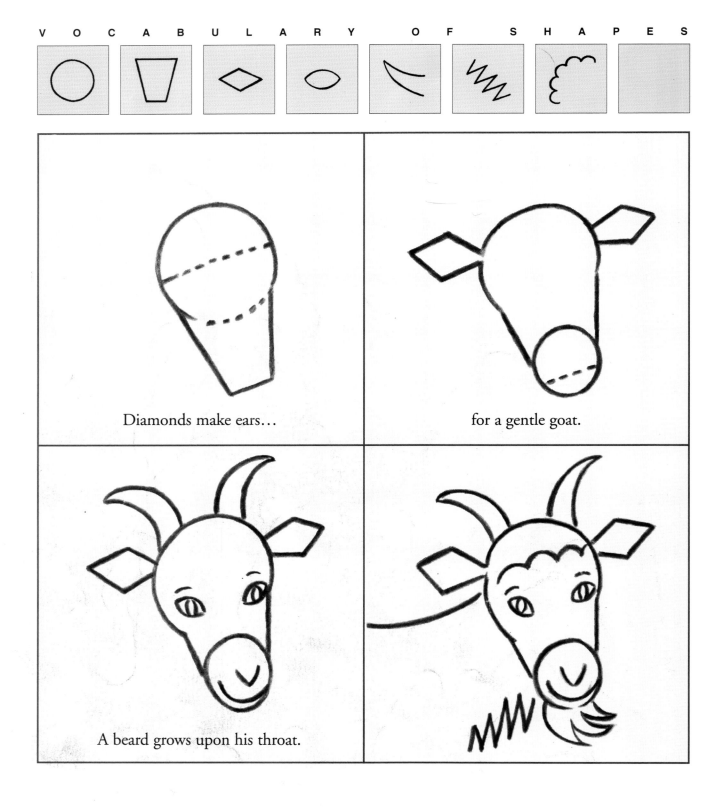

Diamonds make ears…

for a gentle goat.

A beard grows upon his throat.

Goat

Half-circles make the sheep…

look right. Her fleece is…

like a cloud of white.

Sheep

The chicken's feet are…

made of sticks.

Behind her follow little chicks.

Chicken

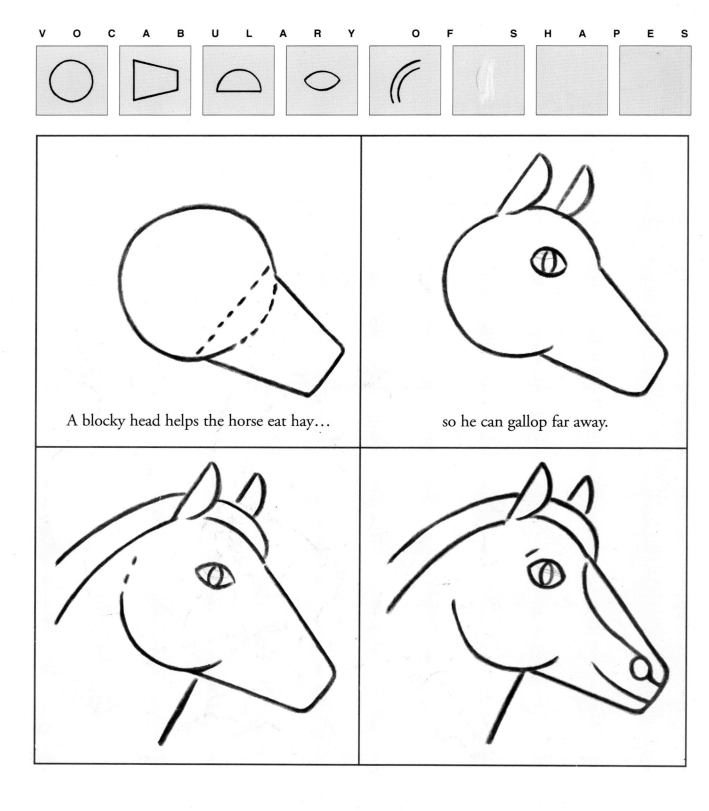

A blocky head helps the horse eat hay...

so he can gallop far away.

Horse

With a triangle beak,

she honks and roams…

around her
barnyard
home.

Goose

The round rooster...

that you drew...

now sings
cock-a-doodle-doo!

Rooster

Milking cows and feeding pigs are common farmyard chores.

But if you've drawn a farm of animals, you've done the task that's yours.

Draw-along fun for children!

With the "I Can Draw" Series, kids ages 6 and up will have hours of fun drawing amazing pictures of all the things they like best—animals, cartoons, creepy creatures, race cars, and more. Each book is full of colorful step-by-step illustrations with easy-to-follow instructions that explain how to draw almost anything by starting with the basic shapes kids already know, such as circles, squares, triangles, and ovals. Each 40-page book includes 8 pages of grid paper.

More step-by-step fun for young artists!

Our "I Can Draw" Drawing Kits come with an instruction book and all the materials kids need for drawing their favorite subjects. Each kit includes colored pencils, sharpener, eraser, and grid paper pad. These handy kits make great gifts for home, school, or travel.

For a free catalog, write to Walter Foster Publishing, 23062 La Cadena Drive, Laguna Hills, CA 92653. Or call (800) 426-0099.